Mother & Son

A Book of Poems and Other Writings

By

Jo Ann Sumbry
and
Gerald D. Griffin

ISBN: 1-4140-2445-2 (e-book)
ISBN: 1-4140-2443-6 (Paperback)

This book is printed on acid-free paper.

1stBooks – rev. 12/05/03

I would like to dedicate my portion of this book to almighty God for His many blessings and for giving me the opportunity to serve as His messenger.

To my parents, the late Rev. James and Mrs. Carrie Lee Sumbry for instilling me with love and Christian morals, values, principles, and standards. May they both rest in peace.

To my son, Gerald, whom I love so very much. I am very proud of his many achievements and the awards he has received since age three and a half.

Jo Ann

Thank you God for being my heavenly father.

Mom, you are the greatest.

Love,
Gerald

Table of Contents

Introduction

This book consists of the first collection of poems and writings by Jo Ann Sumbry and her son, Gerald Griffin. The authors' writings are based on their passion for writing and the experiences they have encountered over the years. Jo Ann and Gerald are God spirited and are greatly concerned about others' well-being.

Not often do parents and their children grow together and form a relationship that lasts from childhood through adulthood. Jo Ann Sumbry and her son, Gerald, are an exception. Since Gerald was two years old, his mother bonded with him to help him to become the best of the best. They have always been inseparable. When you would see one, you would see the other. Of course, there were occasions when Jo Ann had to stand back and allow Gerald to be coached by his father, but there were only a few such occasions during Gerald's childhood and adolescent years. For the most part, it was *mother* and *son* fighting the battles with God on their side.

Jo Ann and her son, Gerald, began getting really serious about their writings when Gerald was in the 7th grade. As the years passed by, Jo Ann and Gerald continued to write and put together their best writings. These are included in this book. We hope you will be inspired by their writings to release some of your own inner feelings through words.

> May God Forever Bless You
> And You Will Be in Our Prayers
>
> Jo Ann Sumbry and
> Gerald D. Griffin
>
> Mother and son

Mother

Jo Ann Sumbry and Gerald D. Griffin

Who am I really?

Who am I really?
There are days that my soul says, "I'm not sure!" Then
I say, Why?
But my spirit says, "You are my child, made in the
very image of me.
Do not be deceived by the enemy when questioned,
"Who am I really?"
Speak out and say, "I really am God's child made in
his own image."
"I am. Really!"

August 18, 2002

Jo Ann Sumbry

We Are Almost There

We are almost there,
Hardship and struggles are everywhere.
So don't give up on the journey,
For at the end there is great joy
For you and for me.

We are almost there
Grab someone's hand and hold on tight
Our battle is almost over,
Soon, very soon we will not have to fight.

Dedicated with love to all my co-workers – May 2002

Jo Ann Sumbry

I Must Go On

I must go on in Jesus' name,
All of my days on earth may not be the same.
With Jesus as my refuge and my guide,
In Him will I trust and abide.

I must go on with my Christian journey,
For eternal life, my Father, is promised to me.
I will hold fast and have faith in God,
Although this road may become extremely rough,
And hard.

I must go on and love others as Christ loves me
And remember that He died at Calvary.
So all of us would be free.
I must go in!

To Mary and your church family,
God Bless you all!

Minister Jo Ann Sumbry
February 2002

We Must Go On

Though times seem hard and rough,

We must go on.

Our paths are filled with problems that are tough,

We must go on.

We may grow tired and weary, but there is an inner light you see.

We must go on.

Hold on to your goals and never let them go.

For the future has much to offer, and one day you will see and you

will know.

But remember – we must go on.

God Is My All and All

God, my Heavenly Father, is my all and all.

He picks me up when I fall.
I love him, my heavenly Father.
His Son, Jesus Christ, and His
Divine Holy Ghost.

However, I know that he loves me
the most.

You may ask how do I know.
My answer to you is the Bible tells me so.

Yes, God is my all and all.

I love Him so much and
I thank Him for answering my every call.

Thank you God for being my all and all!

August 17–18, 2002
Jo Ann Sumbry

Love?

Many people say that they love, but what is love? Is it a feeling or desire? Is it something that does something? How do we know when it is love? Can we live love or see it? Should we talk about it or carry out plans to help formulate it? Can love really be defined? If so, can we define it by expression or demonstration?

Is love what love does? If so, how? If not, why? Are you in love? Do you love? Can you love? How much should you love?

Love? Maybe or maybe not?

August 18, 2002

People

People are different.
Some have initiative.
Some are givers, some are not.
Some have great attitudes, the right minds, and the right spirits.
These are the people who are genuine and true.
These are the people who you can count on.
These are God's chosen people.

May 28, 2002

Jo Ann Sumbry and Gerald D. Griffin

#1 Son

He's #1 to me,
I love him dearly.
I make my concern known
To him each day.
By the things I do
And the words I say.
Who can this person be?
Why, of course, my only son,
He's #1 to me.

September 2, 1994

LET'S TAKE A STAND FOR OUR CHILDREN

Let's take a stand for our children.
We must render them our support on a daily basis.
For our leadership is most important to each of them;
Whether they are rich or poor, high achievers or low.

Let's take a stand for our children.
If they decide to choose the path of failure,
We must not hesitate to say, "Stop! You are going the wrong way."
We must be good role models for our children of tomorrow;
It is our duty as adults to guide them.
Praise them when they do good, and correct them when they make mistakes.

L — ove them!
E — njoy them as they grow older!
T — each them daily
S — upport them!

T — alk to them!
A — sk them questions!
K — eep their minds occupied with positive thoughts!
E — ncourage them to do good!

A — ssist them in their studies!

S — ignal to them when they're wrong!
T — rain them to be the best of the best!
A — llow them to share their thoughts with you!
N — ever discourage them!
D — emand that they have discipline and respect!

F — orgive them when they make errors!
O — ffer them help constantly!
R — espect their thoughts and ideas!

O — rganize a setting for learning to take place!
U — nderstand their needs!
R — ender help to them when needed!

C — are for them as if they were your own children!
H — onor their thoughts!
I — nclude their ideas as often as possible!
L — ead them in the right direction!
D — iscover their gifts and talents!
R — ejoice with them when they do good!
E — xcite them with great ideas!
N — urture them!

Ms. Jo Ann Sumbry
March 23, 1998

I HAVE A SPEECH FOR YOU TODAY

I have a speech for you today
only a few words I will say.
Do your best at home and school
follow and obey every rule.

Love your classmates, mom, dad, sister,
brother and teachers too!
And remember that they also love you.

I have a speech for you today,
always complete your schoolwork
before you go to play.

Hard work and being nice will help
you to be your best.
Never, never worry about failing a test.

I have a speech for you today,
and it ends something like this.
You're the greatest kids I know,
each of the teachers told me so.

I am delighted and glad to be with you today,
To honor you in this very special way.
Happy Honors Day, students in Grades K–3.
Being your guest today is most exciting to me!

I hope to visit you again,

13

Please call or write and let me know when.

Dedicated to K-3 Students
by
Ms. Jo Ann Sumbry
Guest Speaker, K-3 Honors Program

She Left First, He Left Next

They were both feeble and in pain.
They, each of them, fought a good
fight, but their time was up.
She left first, then he left next
one after the other, they left. The
pain of losing them almost caused
another death.

Dear God, be with him and
her and their child on earth.
For the child will never forget
that she left first, then he left next.

August 18, 2002

Jo Ann Sumbry

In loving memory of Mama and Daddy
You left me one after the other – Mama in March 1995 and Daddy in
September 1996.
I miss you!

A Family Built with a Foundation of God's Love

Dedicated to my family
Family Reunion, July 7, 2002

Our family is built with a
    foundation of God's love
For God kept all of us
    safe as He watched from heaven above.

How do we know that God has given us
    this sold and secure foundation?
Our spirit tells us so,
    which is God's creation.

Therefore, our family must remember not to stray
    from God and sin,
For if we do, we must
    be disciplined.

God's love for our family extended to Christ dying on the Cross at Calvary
    We thank Him on this day that we are free.
God's love through Jesus Christ, His only Son,
    will be the foundation of our Family for years to come.

by
Jo Ann Sumbry

I Give the Greatest Gift Because I Teach

I give the greatest gift because I teach.

I expect each of my students to have goals they desire to reach.

I know that students will not all learn at the same time, but

I work with them and encourage them to be strong.

I tell them, "The road you travel may not always be easy, but you must

remain on it to the end."

It is with endurance, patience, faith, and courage; this is where their

rewards will begin.

Many times students ask, "Why do you teach?"

My answer to them – "It is a gift from God. It is my calling."

T – ake them on the path of righteousness.

E – ncourage them to do good and be kind-hearted.

A – llow them to correct their mistakes.

C – omfort them when they are in distress.

H – elp them in time of need.

by
Jo Ann Sumbry
Sunday, July 7, 2002

Wonderful People

Some people do things to be honored and recognized.

Some people do things **because** they need to be done.

Some people do things just for the sake of doing them.

You are different; you are a servant to mankind.

Unlike other people, your light shines bright as the midnight star.

The things you do for others are done with warm spirit and kindness.

The world is a better place because of people like you.

Jo Ann Sumbry
May 28, 2002

A message from Ms. Sumbry

Dear Students:

I am honored to say that this has been a great school year. I have enjoyed working with each of you. As you begin to approach the next school year, please remember that you are the best.

Best

Yes, you are the best to me!
No matter what others may say or see.
High achievers, great students, great readers.
Nothing but the best!
So, go on be what you want to be!
Doctor, lawyer, nurse, teacher, or even someone
famous on TV!
It doesn't matter what career you decide,
I will stand by you and smile with pride.
For you are the best,
Nothing but the best to me.

Sincerely yours,

Jo Ann Sumbry,
Your Principal

Jo Ann Sumbry and Gerald D. Griffin

Patient

*Dedicated to Dr. Eunice Bonsi and all of my Summer Youth College
Students of Tuskegee University*

To be patient is to be kind and true.

Trust in God and He will see you through

Each day will be different you see.

Problems may come your way, but say

"Lord, help me, your child, through this day."

Do go ahead: be strong, loving, cheerful, obedient too,

And watch as God's Holy Spirit comes through.

If times are hard right now, take a breath or two;

And pray, pray, pray to be patient and wait

On your prayer to be granted from our Almighty Above.

– Jo Ann Sumbry
– July 10, 2003
9:10 a.m.

I Fear God Alone!

I fear no one but God.
Although your earthly position is of
great significance to man.
You don't frighten me because I fear God alone!
You may trip me as I walk along the path,
but I will still prosper
You can ridicule me, or even call me names
It is okay because I will only fear God!

August 18, 2002

Jo Ann Sumbry and Gerald D. Griffin

TO: Dr. Eunice Bonsi and
the Summer Youth College Students
at Tuskegee University

DATE: *Revised Summer, 2003*

TO SAY "THANK YOU"

To say "thank you"
for what you do,
Hello, Good Morning,
and I'm proud of you.

To say "thank you"
means so much,
A happy smile, a pat on the back,
or to say, "Hey, I like that."

To say "thank you"
must come from the heart.
Go ahead, say it. Begin now or you may never start.

To say "thank you" …

By Jo Ann Sumbry

Original version written
November 22, 1994

Dedicated to my staff, teachers, and students.

Jo Ann Sumbry

IT HAPPENED TO ME

Living in this world of violence, fear, and pain, we often hear from time to time how many people are physically and mentally abused in their homes. I've often wondered about the people that have committed these crimes.

Many questions have crossed my mind: "Could some of these terrible things happen to me?" Being pleasant as I greet new and familiar faces each day, I never thought that I would be assaulted in my home. But I was wrong; it did happen to me.

I'll probably never forget how it happened. I hope this fear will diminish as the days go by, or as I write and share with my friends here in Sun Belt III, the most tragic time of life.

It happened on Monday, July 11, 1983, approximately 2:30 a.m. I can remember getting ready for bed that Sunday night, not a feeling of worry on my mind. I turned off the lights in my bedroom, and eased myself into my soft, comfortable bed.

After being asleep for awhile, I turned over as I usually do, to the other side of my pillow. My blurry eyes opened slightly and sensed this large, vague shadow looming over me. I could feel the presence of another person in the room with me.

I jumped up, screaming with fear. I then felt something pressing against my right shoulder. At this time I saw something silver pointing toward the upper left side of my body. While all this was happening, I continued to scream for my mother to come to my rescue.

During this time, I was also struggling with an unknown, vicious body. I remember catching this silver thing (it was a large knife) with

23

my left hand, it came between my pointing finger and my thumb (in the center portion).

At the time, I felt no pain – only fear. I held the knife with a passion; it was like a dreadful nightmare. My screaming became more severe. I said, "Mama-a-a-a-, Oh, Mama, there's a man in our house, please help me." I can remember calling God too, because it was He and He only that could really save me.

My mother finally heard my call and ran into the hallway where there was light. She was screaming and shouting in fear, as I pleaded to her not to come into my room. My only intentions were to scare this human monster away. Mama continued to scream for help in her bedroom doorway, begging this criminal to leave her daughter alone. When he realized that I had been injured, he released my body and fled quickly on foot from my bedroom. Again, I called my mother. I screamed, "Mama, Mama, get back, please get back."

Mama was standing, slightly behind her half-cracked door waiting to see the appearance of this man. She said that he had his right hand covering his face as he ran rapidly down our hall, escaping through our opened back door, which had been locked before we retired for bed.

After hearing the back screen slam loudly, we felt sure that he was out of the house. We ran quietly out the front door to our next door neighbor's house. At this time, I began to see the blood pouring from my left hand along with a large cut that stood open.

Police officers and paramedics were soon at our rescue. I was questioned about the incident but unable to give any information on the facial features of the criminal. My mother and I only remembered the light-blue shirt that he was wearing. I was taken to Cobb Memorial Hospital in Phenix City for treatment of my injury.

After being stitched up and waiting several hours for the numb feeling to leave my hand, I thought and cried to myself.

This tragedy upset my entire family. Many of them were there with me while I sat and waited for the physician to tell me some news about my hand. The physician was in and out of the room checking my wound. When he entered the final time, he gave me a form directing me to the Medical Center of Columbus, Georgia. I was hospitalized for three days and surgery was performed on my left hand.

After surgery, I was dismissed for home, thinking at all times about my fears of returning there. My fears are still within me, but hopefully with God's help, my loved ones, and my dear friends in Sun Belt III, I will overcome these fears.

At this point, my mind is at ease from reading a biblical view from St. John, Chapter 14, Verse 1: "Let not your heart be troubled." I plan to read this verse from time to time when I feel weak, troubled, or down. I do believe that this ghostly feeling will fade away slowly, but I'll probably always feel some of the pain and fear, and wonder to myself, "Why did it happen to me?"

Jo Ann Sumbry and Gerald D. Griffin

Son

Black Streak

As someone sings
Their personal version of the
Star Spangled Banner,
I recognize that I am only
A Black Streak on a White Wall.
Only me, there alone.
When I examine
The Black Streak on the White Wall,
A lovely person is in sight, but just out of
my range.
A Black Streak on a White Wall
Reflects all inside shadows.
A Black Streak on a White Wall —
Always alone with that lovely shadow
Haunting him.

Gerald Griffin
7th Grade

Forged words

Words forged
in my heart
vibrate

through phonemes on
my tongue
that sends resonances of
matters of the mind into
the open countryside populated
merely by
the freedom of injustice
that forces my body
to ring with pain
and develop faith
from that darkness in the sun.

Gerald Griffin

Interrupted

With screaming aches of a ripped
heart, I sit.

Stagnant and silent,
quiet and weeping, trusting.

Excuse me.
No – excuse
you.

It's time you are excused;
I've been holding my head down for way too
long now.
It's time to release that raging blaze in me.

You've said your peace; let me yell my
war.

Hear me. Hear this.
No longer will I accept
second place.
I'm finally listening to old mothers
that held and lost babies to your power.

I retract it. Your power just got
cut off, blown out: you've been
interrupted.

Good old Wallace is asleep now: dreaming
his nightmare (my fantasy) of black,
getting red and refusing to wait
any longer.

Tell Miss Loretta

that her driver has driven off.
He couldn't wait for her tips
and small gifts anymore.
This time he had to go claim
his own prize.

Wake up, Sir:
Fannie left work today
and your dishes and children
need to be cleaned.
I guess you better get to scrubbing.
She ain't coming back;
something about a prize
her Momma had her eyes on long ago.

Today, victory is mine.
I've unshackled my mental chains
and realized the battles have already been fought:
(you sure can keep secrets)
The Zulu speared those British;
Ethiopia crushed Mussolini;
Turner burned down your farms,
killed your men;
Haitians conquered your French;
Malik spoke and acted upon the
simple truth;
No I just scream it.

Excuse you *(smile)*:
Victory's won.

Gerald Griffin

for all blind

When the painter pictured the wall,
it cried from homeliness until it bled green.
The excited artist knew it was alive when wet,
tearing spots sprouted from the once gray,
flat wall. And then the blonde
erupted to life, waiting for her dress

composed of ivory and sunflower yellow. That dress,
perfectly tailored for the young maiden, staring into the way,
still blank. The architect's work lacked the blonde
that reveals too much too often. The designer stared at the green
painter who believes art is expressed with hints of gray
captured in the motion of wet

fingers diving into the secretions of fear that wet
all-dry, doggish day. The players of the portrait had to dress
center only to make sure they were aligned away from the uniformity
in gray.
That poor painting cried, hiding all emotions in the wall.
Then it screamed through green.
The beautifully decorated blonde

wept out of sorrow for her lost blonde
sisters she had yet to meet – all formed from the wet,
frenzied fingers of the painter of green.
Everyone, everything had a dress,

33

an outfit, a distinctive wear that flavored the wall
with red-cinnamon-sweet, bitter-lemon yellow, competing with the
gray-

steel, putrid taste of austerity. Determined to kill gray,
the colors blended and bended to form lively fields for the young
blonde.
All these things on the wall
occurred at times when only the wet-
fingered ones let their minds loose and stopped to dress
the bandages of empty dream-scenes. So green

splashed its way onto the wall. Green
trickled down and bled into the hidden fractures in gray.
The blond smiled in the French lace dress
that the painter thought suitably fitted her. Blonde
on blonde on the green on gray for the wet
on dry and obtuse wall.

Once a crying canvas, now a show of blondes,
Forever a gray stone, suddenly transformed into a rich, wet
place to inspire the dress of the dreariest wall.

— Gerald Griffin

Diane:

Like grandfather's hilly farm,
all green with lust:
lying and wading with the
dandelions –
anticipating spreading your
jealously and obsession
with your spurious spores.

Morning, Di.

Inside,
grandmother has
brewed coffee specially
flavored with cream
that once dripped
from the cow that witnessed
your act of thievery.

Oh, Diane.

Walking up the stairs,
I see your heels on the
flight above:
Boldly stepping into
the door that all
too often liberates you from
a world restrained by
commitment and
hearts-fulfilled.

In your well-deserved
cell, framed with bounds of
honesty

Jo Ann Sumbry and Gerald D. Griffin

you lie; as you
flap your legs
those evil seeds
fall
to the metallic floor
polished with that
adultery in your heart.

Mourning Di: stolen love dies so quickly.

— Gerald Griffin

Church-folk Humility

Can't you see?

Look!

Yeah,
It ain't me.

Don't be shy; make yourself at home.
Relax and sit for a while.

Oh baby, don't mess with that there, that's my good set.

You hear it, yeah. Shush,
Hear and feel the Word.

I'll hold that now baby, that's my good Bible. Amen.

Why you look at me?
I told you; it ain't me.

That's my
testimony.

Every victory can't be won alone,
Sure my name's on the plaque but
There's more to it
Than simply that.
To prescribe every accomplishment to me,
To sit down and praise me –

Child stop now, I'm just too grateful; Don't look at me, not me. Not
even about me.

Relax, listen, sip tea

And eat.

Partake.

Wake up and realize:
It ain't me;

Yes, you're right: it ain't you;
It's the only One that can
like no other could.

On My Own

"*On My Own*"

By: Gerald Griffin

While walking into the cramped room, a sense of sadness enveloped my body. A nightmarish omen had seemed to make itself very visible to me. I was witnessing my grandmother's long journey to death.

And I was just lonely: I was losing my best friend.

Driving up to the nursing home was not easy for my mother, grandmother, or me. My mother was worried that it would seem as if she were abandoning the very person who had given her life. My grandmother was not familiar with a restricted lifestyle at all; she was a full-spirited woman who liked to feel free to do as she pleased. And I was just lonely: I was losing my best friend.

The memories of my grandmother giving me pancakes and jelly flashed across my mind. The sound of her playing the piano and guitar filled my ears. But what I remembered most about my grandmother was the advice she had given me about life. She told me to never let anyone know everything about me, as she said it, "Don't let your left hand know what your right hand is doing." She taught me to take pride in myself and my work. She was a wise woman, and I absorbed everything she had taught me.

But now she was not her usual self. She could no longer play the piano or the guitar. She was quiet and showed no expressions. She was no longer talkative or happy. Sometimes, on the good days, she would get very excited to see my mother, but most of the times she just sat there. When Alzheimer's took its deadly swing, she didn't even remember who I was, her favorite grandchild, her only grandson. On the worst days, she didn't recognize her only living child, my mother.

My mother cried. She cried a lot. But somehow, my mother managed all this emotional stress, plus raising me, and the duties of an administrator at a middle school. People were so busy telling my mother about their problems that they didn't even consider listening or asking about hers. My mother had to separate her personal life completely from her professional one. When she felt as though she had to cry, she had to smile. When she felt as though it was time to give up, she had to remember that many children and adults were counting on her for guidance. She had to evolve into a really strong woman.

However, this really strong woman had suddenly become worn out. My grandmother's health was declining and I was just beginning the Terrible Teens. She had an ex-husband that did not even care about her problems. What he had failed to recognize was that her problems were also mine.

When my mother told me my grandmother had died, it did not affect me that much. However, the time I almost broke down was when I realized that her death would forever change my life. I had no counselor nor comforter; the person I had admired most would be gone forever. I had to comfort and counsel myself. I had to learn to call on God through Gerald, not Grandma. Her wise sayings will always stay in my mind, heart, and soul, only now I have to interpret and act upon them on my own.

A Quest for Wisdom:

An introduction to the featured articles in "Perspectives 1999,"
a student magazine of artistic and written composition

By: Gerald Griffin, Editor

Stay calm. It'll be okay. I know it is time to leave for school, and you can't find your car keys. But that's okay; we're here to help. No, they're not in your pocket; yet, we've dedicated an entire magazine to your never-ending act – the act of searching.

Searching has been the fundamental tool for humans. When people have questions, they search for answers. As people find answers, they search for proof. And when people have proof, they search for ways to use the answers to help society. Searching gives people knowledge; searching provides wisdom.

Follow the drawings of people searching; they are a reflection of you. Like you, they are questioning problems, finding solutions, and gaining wisdom. Our "search for imagination" will begin the quest for wisdom. It will have you questioning exactly where ideas come from. The next search will provide some ideas – only to involve more questions about the decisions in the fashion world. Searches that people go through during the transition from high school to the "real world" and "college life" follow. These searches will provide a portrait of making it on your own, a must for obtaining wisdom.

After obtaining the tools for wisdom (questions, answers, and perseverance), you must be able to use it. Wisdom not shared is ignorance. Therefore, we continue our quest with a search for acceptance. This article examines the desire to be socially accepted. This is a desire that can definitely hinder the application of wisdom. After this search, we will discuss technology and the application of science and knowledge. Continuing the quest for wisdom, we search for peace. Peace must be instilled before wisdom can produce an effect. The next article discusses how people use their search for "a topic" to create literature.

Jo Ann Sumbry and Gerald D. Griffin

The next articles show how you must deal with wisdom: new wisdom can lead to destruction if not used properly. Our search for understanding depicts why we should rid ourselves of misconceptions to see the truth. The article describing our schools' integration shows how wisdom can replace evil with care. Our final search is the search for God. It is an eternal search that can lead to answers that cannot be proven; we must have faith. Should everything be proven? Don't answer now. Wait until you have your new-found wisdom. Then you'll have the answers to everything – right?

Colors of the Inner Room

by: Gerald Griffin

Red spoke boldly upon the muted wall. The sun moved slowly up the window and timidly pressed its shadow into the spotty dull-grey carpet. Time was moving – slowly. The warm blanket was comforting. It made the soul feel at home, even at times when the body felt ten thousand miles removed. It would be a day of crisp endings and classy beginnings. As Ralph smelled the moist collards, rain began to drizzle upon his window.

"A charge to keep I have," Momma moaned. "I have a God to glorify." Ralph loved it when Momma sang; her voice roused his soul. She was always singing, reading the Bible, praying, attending Sunday School, healing the sick, or interpreting tongues. People thought she was so spiritual. They claimed her obedience to God was a sacrifice in its own right. All the women in the church idolized her. Even Rev. Thomas's wife asked Momma to pray for her. Momma had everything.

"I ain't going," Ralph said in muffled tones from under his snug blanket.

"You knows you're wrong, it's your duty boy. It's a father's—"

"Ain't got no father."

The words slithered with disgust from his tongue. They cut and comforted him at that exact moment. He couldn't go. He wouldn't. His only duty was to God; Momma said that herself. Ralph didn't owe anyone anything, especially not that man. He didn't even know him. Besides, that old man was stiff now; he couldn't feel a thing.

Not having a father did not bother Ralph much. In fact, he preferred it that way. He loved his life, the simplicity. He was graduating at the top of his class, he had obtained a basketball scholarship to Duke, and he had too many friends to count. What could a father have provided that he did not already have? Ralph had no need for that complication. He had no need to realize the complication of owning or relating to a "father." That idea had been foreign to him ever since birth. Ralph lived his life.

Ralph smirked to himself. He was living – well. He was looking forward to the party tonight celebrating the basketball team's advancement to play-offs. All the local papers predicted that this might be the year of a state championship for them. He looked at his hand. It did seem to be missing a little gold that a state championship ring would be able to provide. He would have plenty to celebrate tonight. Thank goodness he had finished his English assignment yesterday. Tonight would be a late, crazy night. Ralph felt like superman.

Ralph rose up. "I ain't going," he said brashly.

"I'm not asking Ralph; I'm telling. You are gonna give your respect – and don't you say you ain't got none; you'd best find it soon. Get up, get dressed, and come out here and help me. This ain't easy for me neither. I don't need this. I don't need you acting up today. I just can't—"

"Who said I'm *acting up*? If it's not so easy, then why do you want to do it? I didn't ask for this. Darn you!" The drizzle became a storm.

She had had enough. He was going and there would be no further arguing. "Boy, what did you say?"

"I said I ain't going," he spoke so coolly.

"Oh, yes you are." The intensity of Momma's voice and spirit quickly manifested into her big, black hand slamming Ralph's head directly into the wall. Her strength was overpowering. His breath seemed to depart his body. He gasped, thirsting for air. Ralph's eyes caught his mother's and the flowing tears crawling down her cheeks. Her breaths were slow and irregular; her body sank deep into his old carpet as she fell to her knees.

Her dark eyes peered deeply into Ralph. Each sight of him was a beautiful reminder of God's unending love for her. Yet, his countenance always tormented her soul. His existence was a perpetual reminder. The way his voice would rise and sharply fall prompted memories of her rapist's husky voice. It was an awful feeling knowing that she would never be able to forget such a terrible event. Even if she could manage to repress the memory to somewhere beyond the conscious mind, Ralph was the shovel unearthing all the pain, agony, and hatred she felt. Living was hard.

She had thought about suicide immediately after the rape. She could not imagine living as a fouled woman. Often, she thought that was God's signal for her death. She could not image Him placing such a burden on her. Was she not faithful to Him? She thought she did her fair share of Christian work. She was an exemplary woman in Christ, right? She began questioning everything. Next, she considered abortion; but, that would be murder. No Christian could ever do that and remain in God's glory.

Momma prayed. She prayed hard every day and fasted for three weeks. She wanted to hear from God; she wanted answers. But she heard none. God had given her a baby; yet, all she thought of was that her son looked too much like his father. She could feel his face in Ralph. It was as if he had possessed her son; he always had control over her.

After taking time to breathe, Ralph crawled out of the speckled sheets and stumbled to the bathroom. Momma always had the bathroom looking, feeling, and smelling like a fresh rose garden. She always layered the harsh smell of bleach and glass cleaner with the fresh pickings from her garden. Cleanliness was not only next to Godliness: it was her hobby. She swept and mopped every day.

Momma cleaned everything. Ralph touched his left cheek where Momma had slapped him. It was sore. There was no blood.

As he washed his face, he looked up and the mirror showed him the bruise. He saw the boy that was supposed to overcome the obstacle of lost paternity. Wasn't he supposed to be a man by now? He had joined the boy scouts in middle school. Next month, he would be an Eagle. He had been going to basketball camp every summer since five. He had dated the finest cheerleader and learned to chug a beer in seventeen seconds. Ralph had even read *GQ, Men's Fitness,* and *Sport Illustrated* to know how to dress and train as all successful men do. But his soul only showed that little boy always waiting for Momma. After he finished washing his face, he glanced at his Nautica cologne bottle. Now, its fragrance seemed useless.

Momma never really had a job except for Church secretary. It wasn't that she was rich but always sick. No place would ever hire her; she missed too many workdays due to backaches, stomach turns, headaches, and severe rheumatoid arthritis. On off-days from the internist, neurologist, or chiropractor, Momma would walk back and forth in her garden of roses. Just roses.

"Why should I go?"

"Because he was your father; yes, you have a father."

"I know. But I didn't know him. Why would it help me to see him dead?"

"Maybe it wouldn't; but it would help me."

"That doesn't make any sense."

"To you. You're so busy you barely recognize how bad I'm hurting sometimes."

"Momma, you know I love you."

"Then you'll come?"

"What?"

"I need this, him to be over. My memories have haunted me since he raped me. It's been hurting me since then."

"Then you should go – have that closure you need; it would only hurt me."

"But he lives in you." Her eyes opened wide and her head fell down.

Ralph's ears burned and his soul bled. It had been so easy to hate, so easy to be contemptuous. But now, he could only hate himself. His enemy lived in him; he realized his father haunted Momma through him. He couldn't live like that. Life suddenly became hard.

"No!" Ralph screamed. Tears flooded his eyes and his spirit felt like drowning. His eternal pain, the sudden guilt all rushed over his body as his fragility sent him to his knees. "Oh, God."

Momma placed her self by Ralph. He was weeping from inside. Her hurt, her anger and disgust had crippled her son. She had been doing the haunting. She took herself to that place of hatred, she felt so red inside. It had been eating away at her and Ralph all this time. How blind and deaf was she? God has sent her the answer to her prayers from long ago: he had sent Ralph. He was her new beginning; he was a sign that life had and could begin again. All that was before had been forgiven, forgotten – erased and lost to the emptiness of time.

"I'm not going either. He's been dead for years now."

Violence had happened. Love had occurred and shined through. There were no more questions of duty or responsibility. Ralph spoke no more of not having a father. All Ralph knew was that his Momma was there with him, and they both loved each other deeply.

The rain poured a bit harder and began to flood the area in the backyard where the rose garden was. Momma frowned a bit. Ralph simply smiled. He knew next season's roses would be the prettiest ever.

A Dream That Became Reality

Today's society is filled with so many different cultures which provide totally different lifestyles for a vast amount of people. There are people from big cities and small cities, undeveloped and developed nations, and families with low standards and high. I just happen to come from a well-developed nation, a small town, and a family that has given me extremely high standards.

My name is Gerald Griffin and I just happen to strive for excellence, which just happens to come with uniqueness (or so I am told). My main objective in life is to prepare myself for future opportunities. Therefore, I place my academic studies before co-curricular activities such as chorus and Interact Club. I must admit that sometimes I do get really involved in the band and our Student Government Association; then my mom reminds me to slow down and take things one step at a time.

My mother and I have a really strong bond that I believe no one on Earth could break. Sometimes we sit and talk about life and the many obstacles that one must go through to be successful; other times we just sit and talk about movies, books, poetry, and life. She has raised me to trust my instincts; she has taught me many morals and values to base my decisions upon. I not only love my mother, but I also love the lessons of life she has taught me.

My mother has lived by determination and she has instilled in me this great trait that will get me through any circumstance. Many of my teachers do not believe how determined and dedicated I am (for with true determination comes dedication). They believe that all advanced students are out for only one thing: the grade. No only do I want to truly learn, but I want to apply my skills so I can become a better person and help others. I have volunteered my time by tutoring peers at my high school, and I have volunteered at a local intermediate school to tutor children there. Determination not only helps me grow; it also influences the ones that I help.

The Summer Honors Programs for High School Sophomores will indeed give me a taste of real college life. My responsibility and maturity will be exemplified upon acceptance in this program. I hope to increase my level of achievement and gain knowledge that will be useful in my future education. This program will give me the chance to express some of my creative ideals that are limited at school. I believe this Honors Program will prepare me for college.

One of the main reasons I pursued this opportunity to attend this program was to use this program as a "leap" into Cornell. I have done my research and have found out that Cornell has one of the best science programs in the nation. Also, I have been selected as a Minority in Medicine and would love the opportunity to participate in the Summer Honors Program to get acquainted with the university. It would be my sincere delight if I were to be selected as a participant in the Cornell University Summer Honors Program.

Gerald wrote this letter of intent to Cornell University during his sophomore year in high school. On May 25, 2003, Gerald graduated from Cornell University with a B.A. degree in biology, specializing in neurobiology.

Gerald had a dream of one day being a student at Cornell University in Ithaca, New York. Two years later, Gerald's dream became a reality. Gerald is still dreaming. Currently, he is a Graduate student at the University of Pennsylvania School of Medicine. Gerald is dreaming of having his own institute(s) of neuroscience where teaching, learning, and research will take place to help those with mental problems, disorders, diseases, and so on. It is Gerald's dream and hope to have two or more neuroscience institutes in the United States and abroad.

Keep on dreaming, Gerald. More reality is waiting ahead for you!

Love,

Mother

Prologue

I am his mother and he is my son. We
are striving to do our best for God. As
we continue this journey, it is our hope
that others will see Christ Jesus in us.

Mother and Son,

Jo Ann Sumbry and Gerald Griffin

Jo Ann Sumbry and Gerald D. Griffin

About The Author

Jo Ann Sumbry

Jo Ann Sumbry is a born-again Christian and woman of God. Born in Columbus, Georgia and raised in Phenix City, Alabama, Jo Ann is a licensed preacher and Associate Minister at the Saint Luke A.M.E. Church in Opelika, Alabama. She is a former elementary teacher, assistant principal, principal, system-wide curriculum director, and state special-services administrator. She is presently the field-based experiences coordinator, instructor, and university supervisor at Tuskegee University in Tuskegee, Alabama. In addition, Jo Ann is pursuing her Ed.D. in educational leadership at NOVA Southeastern University. She is known by many for being warm-spirited, inspiring, and motivating. Her greatest gift from God is her son, Gerald, co-author of this book.

Gerald D. Griffin

Gerald D. Griffin was born on January 1, 1981, in Columbus, Georgia and raised in Phenix City up to grade five. Like his mother, Gerald has a special God-given spirit about him that touches everyone he meets. Gerald is known by his friends and others as the "perfect" intelligent gentleman. He is blessed with multiple gifts and talents. Gerald graduated from Opelika High School in the top one per cent of his class. In 1996, he was selected to be a participant in the United States Collegiate Wind Band, performing in more than eight countries throughout Europe. He graduated from Cornell University in Ithaca, New York on May 25, 2003 with a B.A. degree in biology, specializing in neurobiology. He was nominated as a National Dean's List Scholar recipient twice consecutively while attending Cornell. Gerald also received many awards and scholarships while attending Cornell. Presently, Gerald is working on his Ph.D. in neuroscience at the University of Pennsylvania School of Medicine. After completing his Ph.D., Gerald anticipates pursuing an M.D. Gerald's greatest gift from God is his mother.

Mother and son
A wonderful team
A perfect example of a
strong family built on love and
blessed by God.

Printed in the United States
33185LVS00003B/38